CW00505491

How to Drive
Operational Excellence

An Integrated and Practical Approach

Dominick Morizio Jr

How to Drive Operational Excellence

An Integrated and Practical Approach

Table of Contents

This book is dedicated to all those supervisors and colleagues from whom I learned so much, and who in their own way influenced the professional and person I am.

Introduction

There are many books available that delve deep into the individual topics I have included in my own book, and I encourage the reader to seek these out – especially if there is an area that he or she believes they need to brush up on or learn about. I have read a substantial number of books on these various subjects over the course of my career and successfully applied all of the tools and theories I will be describing. In fact, many of them I also learned while working for successful companies, and I have experienced firsthand how a company must take an integrated approach to driving operational excellence. This was especially the case during my years at Yum! China.

Upon reflection, though, I realized that it would have been very handy – and certainly more efficient – if I had had material early on in my career that tied these elements together. That is what prompted me to write this book. It is not meant to be a textbook, but a practical approach based on my personal experience in driving operational excellence.

The key to operational excellence can be crystalized as: *having the right people operating in the right culture, doing the right things the right way over time.*

Operational excellence can also be expressed in the following diagram:

I will be discussing each of these elements in the ensuing chapters and providing examples I have experienced or observed throughout my career, but I would like to explain here what I mean by the word "right" in the above definition.

I do not use the term in its moral sense, as in right and wrong or good versus bad, but rather in terms of its secondary meaning, which denotes appropriate, correct or true. What is "right" as it pertains to the operational excellence model very much depends on the business one is in and the operating environment and challenges a company is facing. In the definition of operational excellence, the word "right" can be substituted for its synonym, true.

Definition - Operational Excellence

Excellence is a quality, and it is the manifestation of this quality that makes something or someone outstanding. In other words, it is what makes something or someone better than good, above the rest, or great.

There are two ways of measuring excellence: in relative or in absolute terms. For some, being above the rest or the best in a given class is the aim. The problem with this relative way of measuring excellence is that if everyone else is substandard, or just slightly better than average, while admirable if they are putting forth their best effort, is really not excellence per se unless they really are the best of the best, such as in the Olympics.

One might argue, then, that a more accurate way to measure excellence is in absolute terms. To do this, though, there has to be something to measure against. That is where standards and benchmarks come into play.

In business operations, many aspects of excellence are easy to measure because operations inherently lend itself to measurement. Think of the outcomes in operations, and they are often quite quantifiable. In production, it comes down to the amount and the quality of items produced. In retail, it is more about the number of customers that are served or how much merchandize is sold. Measuring excellence gets harder when it is determined by the quality of customer experience, level of satisfaction or other intangible aspect of business operations where it is more subjective.

The attainment of operational excellence is also greatly determined by the level and quality of execution. In an operational sense, *execution* pertains to the putting-into-effect plans and actions that drive outcomes.

It's not enough to have a great plan or idea, or even the best intentions. It will only mean something if you can execute it and operational excellence can only be achieved through brilliant execution.

There is also a dynamic element to excellence – one that requires work, diligence, perseverance and purpose. It can also be temporary or fleeting. Once a certain level of excellence is achieved, it has to be maintained, or even improved upon. Indeed, those who achieve greatness can maintain excellence over an extended period of time. This can be for a thousand years, as was the case for the Roman Empire, or hundreds of years, as with Mozart's music. Some people may achieve greatness over several decades, including sports professionals like basketball phenomenon Michael Jordan, or Apple in the business world.

But I also want to be clear that what I am writing about is excellence, not perfection, and it is very important to distinguish the two. By definition, *perfection* lacks any defects or flaws. In theory, something, or someone, can be both perfect and excellent, but they don't have to be perfect in order to be excellent.

I would also argue that perfection is unreachable in today's fast-changing and increasingly dynamic business environment, as it takes time, effort and money to attain, and the world does not stand still long enough to do so. By the time perfection is achieved, it won't be long before whatever – or whomever – has been perfected becomes out of date or irrelevant. Also, the costs associated with reaching perfection may not be justifiable in terms of return on investment.

The main reason for this new dynamism in the business world has everything to do with advances and changes in technology, especially mobile technology and social media platforms. Social media and mobile technology have increased the rate at which we communicate and process information, and they have had a democratizing effect. For example, think of companies such as Uber, who use mobile technology to challenge established transportation business models. Through new technology, customers can directly utilize these companies' services and even provide feedback that other customers use to make purchase decisions. Consider this book, too, which I am able to release without the help of a publishing company, which would have been essential less than a decade ago.

In striving for perfection, one can get bogged down in details and become obsessed with the very idea of striving for perfection. So, it's important to remember that we do live in an imperfect world, and that human beings are far from flawless creatures. The Christians believe we are born with original sin, while the ancient Greeks wrote about the sin of pride or hubris; and nowadays, our bookshelves are filled with countless self-help books. We can embrace this imperfection like Japanese Zen Buddhist monks do with the imperfection of their ceramic tea cups in which they have deep appreciation for the defects in the pottery. We can realize that it is because of life's imperfections that we have such diversity in the world, and that life is so interesting.

However, while perfection may be too costly or impractical in the business world, striving for excellence is entirely practical and necessary – especially in an increasingly competitive world. By making a sound effort, not only can organizations and their staff grow and develop, but they can drive wealth, fulfillment and ultimately reach new heights.

The Core – The Right People

By the "right people," I mean qualified and competent management and staff who uphold compatible values with the company culture.

But it all begins with the company founder(s). In short, the company culture stems from their values since they are the ones who recruit and attract the initial leadership team and other employees.

The Chinese have an expression, "If the head is crooked, so too will be the body." For our purposes, this means that if the direction leadership is taking is inaccurate or off the mark, then so too will be the rest of the organization. When evaluating a company for its prospects of operational excellence, the reader can use the content of this book to help determine whether the founders have the right people in place to achieve and sustain operational excellence.

When it comes to planning for operational excellence, one of the best places to look is in the company's organizational structure, followed by the recruitment and staff development procedures that are in place to fill that structure.

There are two books that the reader may reference for additional information on these subjects: *Organizational Behavior: Key Concepts, Skills & Best Practices, 5th edition* by Angelo Kinicki and Mel Fugate, as well as *How To Hire The Right People* by Stan Dubin.

But my opinion is that one of the first steps should be the design of an organizational chart and structure that will set the company up for operational excellence. This includes things such as reporting lines and layers of management, and this will develop based on the size and complexity of the organization, as well as on the specific business. A large company like General Motors will have a much more complex structure than a single Subway store, for example.

But in terms of organizational planning, I have found a few key characteristics that are critical to driving results: 1) executive effective span of control, 2) structural accountability 3) a lean and flat structure

Executives have different levels of energy, capacity for work, tolerance of stress and styles. Each of these factors impacts how effective they are at managing their subordinates. For example, an executive who has learned to incorporate delegation as an important part of their management style will be more effective at managing a larger number of subordinates than an executive who has not mastered the art of delegation. My experience in dynamic situations (that often occur with a crisis in the background) has caused me to believe that the most effective executive span of control for an experienced executive, or someone with at least ten years of experience, is eight direct reports, with a broader range of six to ten depending on the executive's experience and the complexity of the business and current situation.

This will ensure that the right amount of time is spent on managing, coaching and developing the team, and also on enabling the executive to delve into the details in order to achieve outstanding execution.

The second point is to build a structure that fosters accountability. Shortly after I joined the company with the development rights for quick-service sandwich brand Subway in Shanghai, I observed that we were not hitting the budgeted number of new franchise contract sales. After reflecting, we found that the then current business model failed to delegate responsibility to the individual who was specifically accountable for driving the sales of new franchises. In other words, too many people were unsure of their role in relation to the outcome in the structure.

What we did to fix this was change the organizational chart and realign the General Manger of the brand to have direct responsibility. In addition, we also redirected the person beneath him, whose sole responsibility was now to drive franchise sales. Those who had been previously involved were redeployed for other work. We also made sure that the person whose prime responsibility was to drive franchise sales had the right title and was motivated by cash incentives and recognition.

You can guess the end result. Within a few weeks, we had traction, and shortly thereafter we were driving sales in line with our budget. It didn't take long before we actually had a backlog of signed franchisees looking for new locations to open stores.

This example shows the difference a clear reporting line with unambiguous accountability and incentives can make on driving outcomes.

The third point concerns building a lean and flat organization. One of the major benefits of this approach is that it helps control costs by reducing the risk of a bloated bureaucracy, which in turn fosters swift, clear communication and alignment. Most importantly, it allows the leadership to stay much closer to the front line and the customer thus getting clearer information.

As I mentioned at the beginning of this chapter, the complexity and size of the company will dictate the complexity of the organizational chart, but the underlying principles and spirit can still be adhered to in a relevant way. I am including a simple organizational chart as an example, which can form the core of a retail business of between 20 and 200 stores. I say "core" because it can be added to or adjusted as needed, based on the particular business, industry and size of the organization. For example, if the company is engaged in franchising, then a Franchise Development department may be added to the organization. Also, considering my thoughts on span of control, this core model does leave room to make adjustments.

Each of the functions will then be populated with the relevant positions. For example, under the CFO there could be a Tax Manager; there could be a Recruiting Manager under Human Resources; and under the Brand GM or Operations Head there could be a Training Manager.

So, the leader of a given company, who may be the founder or a hired professional, needs to develop an effective organizational structure that will serve as a platform to drive operational excellence by fostering clear accountability, communication and alignment while minimizing costs. Once this structure is set, more detail ought to be added – for example, job descriptions. I will discuss this in greater detail later in the book, in the chapter on tools and process, but for now I want to mention that it is important to write out exactly what each of these positions will entail, what they should achieve and how they relate to others in the organization.

Once the organizational structure and job descriptions are complete, the next task is to start hiring and filling the positions with the right people. This is one of the most time-consuming, difficult, and critical tasks when it comes to setting a company up to achieve operational excellence.

A detailed discussion on the recruiting process is beyond the scope of this book, especially the interview, but an excellent resource on the subject is *Recruiting, Interviewing, Selecting, & Orientating New Employees, Fifth Edition* by Diana Arthur.

I would, however, like to share some personal observations in this regard, as they relate to driving the operational excellence that I have achieved over the course of my career. I have not only been in the role of interviewee during many job interviews, but also the role of interviewer, while building management teams at two companies and hiring dozens of other personnel. In addition, at Yum! China, one of my prime responsibilities as Director of Franchise Development was to sort through thousands of applications, conduct scores of interviews each year and select the most suitable candidates.

Observations on recruiting for operational excellence:

1) Be clear on the skills you need, the style you are looking for and whether you need someone who will grow into the role you are hiring for or someone who is ready for the position but has the potential to grow into a higher-level role. In other words, keep development in mind when you hire your staff. Avoid the trap of trying to fill a vacancy immediately at the expense of considering the development potential of

your new employee. The reason is that it will take time to integrate this employee into your winning culture, and you want to ensure that he or she will remain engaged with their work while this transition occurs and beyond. One great way to keep an employee fired up is through career development, where they will learn new skills and take on more responsibility as time goes on.

2) Be prepared! Unfortunately, I have sat through more interviews than I care to remember where senior executives hadn't adequately reviewed my resume, hadn't organized a proper interview venue or didn't know how to interview.

None of us are born knowing how to interview – this is a skill we must learn. And believe it or not, many companies do not train their executives on how to interview and hire personnel. As I said, hiring the right people is one of the single biggest influencers of driving operational excellence, so it always amazes me when I encounter the issues I am discussing here.

The most important thing is to be honest with yourself. If you were never trained, and if you've never read a book on recruiting and interviewing, get yourself educated – that's the first step you should take to become more prepared.

I'll share an experience of mine from years ago, when I interviewed with the Senior Vice President of an international media company in Shanghai. Naturally, I had arrived at his five star hotel early, but the executive was late. He had also, failed to organize a place for the interview, so we went to his hotel suite which had an extensive living room area. But to my amazement, the executive had left his gym clothes out on the sofa to dry, and he hadn't removed them for the interview, so we sat on the sofa for the interview surrounded by his drying gym clothes. As if this wasn't bad enough, he did most of the talking during the interview. Afterward, I told the headhunter what had happened and that I was not interested in proceeding should anything come of the meeting. This was not an isolated case, mind you, and I have had other interviews with Divisional Vice Presidents of major multinational companies that weren't much better, aside from the fact that there was no "dirty laundry" involved. The more I thought about it, the more I realized that unless they were apathetic or arrogant, the most likely reason for this behavior was that these individuals hadn't been trained on how to recruit and interview. Or, perhaps these cases are a reflection of the company culture and how executives treat people.

The other aspect of being prepared is making sure that if you are interviewing someone, that you have actually reviewed their resume ahead of time and prepared interview questions for areas that you would like to better understand. These could relate to job skills, style or development potential. Since time is often the greatest limitation of an interview, it is counterproductive to waste time asking questions on basic information that is already written out on the candidate's resume. It doesn't make the greatest impression on an interviewee for you or your company, and it doesn't demonstrate respect.

I have been on countless interviews where, based on the interviewer's questions, I could tell that he or she hadn't taken the time to read my resume in advance. It's appropriate to begin an interview with an open question such as, "So, tell me about yourself and your career." Sometimes an interviewer simply wants to see if what you say jives with what you've written down, and to determine whether you are prepared, but it's not acceptable to go into an interview without having thoroughly read through and evaluated a candidate's resume with a specific game plan for what you want to find out; that's not how one hires for excellence.

3) Listen versus talk. I believe that in situations where the interviewer does most of the talking, there is a serious lack of training on how to interview, which is a very common mistake. Again, I've been on many of these type of interviews where the interviewer did most of the talking and I always walked away feeling shortchanged.

During interviews, the only talking I do is to ask questions and provide a brief introduction about the company and the position I'm recruiting for, which ensures the candidate and I are in alignment. Then, at the end of the interview, I answer any additional questions the candidate may have, and I let them know what next steps are. In other words, I leave at least 80% of the talking to the candidate.

The Core – The Right Culture

Since excellence is a quality that requires great effort, there must be underlying values that drive a company or individual to attain and maintain it. The starting point for these values is culture, which is why it is at the core of the operational excellence model.

In defining the word culture, I would say that it is *a composite of a group's beliefs and behaviors, which serves to give it identity and cohesiveness*. In a business sense, company culture defines what an organization does and how it goes about doing so.

Company culture has to start somewhere, consciously or unconsciously, and it is the result of the company's founder(s). Wal-Mart would not be Wal-Mart without its culture, which founder Sam Walton set in motion with his principles and personal style. In short, any company culture is based on the specific values of the founder(s). How fast they move; how they conduct meetings; the quality of their work; who they hire and what qualities they look for in those hires; how they pay and treat their employees and how they value characteristics such as honesty, integrity and hard work all come into play in the underlying culture.

In the previous paragraph, I wrote "consciously or unconsciously" because a founder may be so busy getting things started that he or she never finds time to sit down and explicitly write out a value statement, or even think about what type of culture they want to create. Often, the company culture they perpetuate is an extension of their own personal value system, and they set it into motion just by being themselves. At some point, though, if the organization grows so large and endures it may outlive the founder. It is therefore critical that the culture and values must be explicitly formalized to ensure perpetuity beyond the founder and those who worked with him or her.

In today's fast-changing world, it is common and normal for companies to sell business units, even ones that they started in industries that they pioneered, and enter a new industry especially through acquisition. But what they don't change is their core culture and values. This enables them to remain who they are, to simultaneously capitalize on the good will of the brand and stay dynamic as they reinvent themselves. In short, this lets them continue to prosper.

General Electric is an excellent example of this. GE is one of the largest conglomerate companies in the US, with a diverse portfolio of companies and businesses involved in a myriad of industries such as energy, appliances, financial services, medical supplies, aviation, software and engineering. The company's roots go back to Thomas Edison and the likes of J.P. Morgan from the late nineteenth century. Throughout its one hundred-plus years of existence, GE has bought companies, merged businesses, spun off some business units and sold others.

Recently, the company announced that they are moving their central office from Fairfield, Connecticut to Boston, Massachusetts, as CEO Jeff Immelt expressed a desire for the company to be better positioned in "an ecosystem that shares our aspirations." And one of those aspirations is for the company to be a "top 10 software company" by 2020, a direction it started moving toward in 2011. Immelt and his team chose Boston because they believe the city provides a better "ecosystem" to support the shift. GE can make this transition and refocus because they're not changing the company culture; rather, they're simply changing the businesses they're in.

In short, company culture is the foundation on which a leader must build operational excellence. And it is imperative that the culture and values come to life in the leadership, as the result of their following the "walk the talk" principle. In other words, this means having leadership who lead by example and not just by words.

While this is not an exhaustive list, I believe that the key building blocks of a successful company culture – of a company culture that drives excellence – are the following: *individual and collective accountability, people development and learning, coaching, recognition, discipline with attention to detail and follow-up, strong alignment, mutual respect and empathy in communications.*

Individual and collective accountability is where people feel responsible for their own actions and take pride in what they do. It's what drives people to go the extra mile to get the job done the right way. This sense of accountability has to be valued on the individual level, especially for individuals who work as part of teams. Everyone must pull their own weight in a team to drive outcomes successfully.

This sense of accountability must permeate the company from top to bottom and from the bottom up. From the front line worker all the way to the senior leadership so that the company holds all people accountable for their actions, behavior and outcomes. The idea is that the employees hold themselves accountable and take pride in what they do.

So, much of what we do in today's business world requires collaboration, and technology has changed the way this collaboration is done. There is often less in-the-flesh interaction, what with conference calls, webinars and virtual meetings being the norm now. In order to minimize any negative effects caused by what some consider impersonal interactive formats, it's imperative to sustain a company culture that instills a strong sense of accountability among personnel, and that will help ensure the job gets done.

I would also like to emphasize that my definition of accountability presumes an understanding and appreciation of quality. I presume that this strong sense of accountability entails a sense of pride in producing a quality product, or in providing a quality service. Simply having a culture that emphasizes only accountability but not quality will not deliver operational excellence.

People development and learning is important because it fosters excellence by enhancing skills, performance and intellect. It helps people grow and take on more responsibility, and it will help them become more of an expert in what they do.

By fostering a culture that values learning, we are in a sense encouraging a culture that supports the striving that is necessary to achieve excellence. The learning can take place in ways ranging from in-house seminars and training programs to the establishment of a virtual company library and resource center. It can also take the form of tuition reimbursement for employee education.

But the most important way to foster learning is to ensure an environment where employees feel comfortable asking questions and sharing information. There is nothing more stifling then working in a company where people feel that asking questions is unwelcome and it can be tragic in a sense, because it prevents the passing on of knowledge and know-how among employees.

Out of all the questions that can be asked, there is one generic question that is sure to bring clarity to any issue. It's a simple and short question that consists of just one word – *Why?*

The practice goes that when a person is facing a problem, he or she should ask, "Why?" anywhere from three to five times to get at the root cause of the problem. For example, an Area Manager is confronted with unusually high staff turnover at one of their retail locations. The first "Why?" is, *Why only at this location?* Well, upon closer examination, the Manager discovers that this location is the only one in his area with a newly promoted Store Manager. The second question, then, is, *Why is this new Store Manager having these turnover issues?* And upon further investigation, it turns out that this Store Manager is purposely changing out people, and this has driven up turnover. Digging deeper, the question then becomes, *Why did this Store Manager feel it was necessary to change out so many people?* In a conversation with the Store Manager, she reveals that there were numerous customer complaints and service issues, and they were in the process of making people changes in order to fix the problem and raise the bar of performance. You could stop here and be content that the Store Manager is addressing the problem, or you could continue to ask, "Why?" to gain a deeper level of understanding and explore how the situation came to be in the first place. You may discover a deeper issue that could have a more profound impact on the business. Perhaps you'll uncover that the root cause of the problem is that the company lacks a store-level employee evaluation process or proper hiring tools.

The reason this store stood out in terms of turnover was that this new manager had a strong sense of accountability, and she decided to do something about the problem. The reason why the other stores did not have the same high turnover was because the Store Managers either didn't realize there was an issue or decided to ignore it, or they had already resolved the same problem. By asking, "Why?" and digging deeper to gain clarity in this example, you uncovered an opportunity to drive operational excellence by focusing on improving processes and gained clarity. And it all started with one simple question- *Why?*

Taking this approach also generates opportunities for *coaching*, which is essential when it comes to performance. Coaching is all about guiding, training and motivating people toward a goal; and in our case, that goal is operational excellence.

A coach's style and communication skills determine how effectively he connects with the people he is coaching. So, it is more than just skill, it's very much about style. For those who are interested in learning more, a fantastic book on the subject is *Coaching for Performance: GROWing Human Potential and Purpose - The Principles and Practice of Coaching and Leadership, 4th Edition* by John Whitmore.

In order for coaching to be effective, it must be consistent and purposeful, and so it has to be a part of the company culture and at the forefront of employees' minds when they interact with one another. However, like with everything else, there should be balance, and it cannot be overdone. Coaching, for example, was an integral part of the culture at Yum! China, where almost every interaction was seen as a coaching opportunity. I can tell you that it was overused at times, but it was the cornerstone of a system to build top operations teams in a developing country especially for a company that was opening a new KFC or Pizza Hut on a daily basis consistently for years.

As a leader, walk the talk, and make sure to coach your people and lead by example. Make it part of what you do, and others will follow your lead; they will in turn coach others.

A related topic to coaching is mentoring, and some companies do make use of formal mentoring programs. Other organizations, such as Universities or Associations, also feature mentoring programs. Yum! China had a mentoring program where I served as both a mentor and a mentee, and my college, Bernard Baruch CUNY, has a mentoring program in which I have also volunteered as an Alumni mentor.

In general, a mentoring program is set up with the intention of enabling less experienced members to benefit from the advice and guidance of more experienced individuals. It may entail offering support and insight on navigating company politics or even with career planning, for example. Often, the program is effective because the mentee feels they have someone they can bounce ideas off of and obtain feedback from, and it can really help them boost their sense of confidence. Usually, a company's Human Resources department manages the program, but participants are encouraged to meet regularly on their own, typically on a monthly basis at the very least.

Mentoring helps drive operational excellence because along with coaching, it encourages reflection and guides performance. As referenced in the introduction to this book, *Workplace Mentoring Shea Reference Guide* by Andrew Jones is a great resource if you'd like to learn more about mentoring.

Recognition is important because it is a strong motivator, and it reinforces what type of behavior is valued by an organization. Recognition can be monetary, symbolic (as in a medal) or verbal (as in "great job!"). Companies that strive for excellence have to weave recognition into all parts of their operation.

As mentioned, I spent a portion of my career at Yum! China, where the recognition culture was formalized at every level of the organization and it was highly effective when it came to driving employee engagement and performance. For example, each functional department had its own award that was presented to individuals or entire departments at the company's annual dinner. These awards were symbolic for each presenting department, and they represented an appreciation for outstanding behavior. The Real Estate Development department, for example, presented a special brick trophy each year to someone they believed had helped support new store development and growth. On a day-to-day basis, items like pins could be used for recognition. My department, which was Franchise Development, had a thumbs-up pin that we gave out to employees and franchisees during store visits, for outstanding service and operations. And the company President had his own "Clock Builder" award, which was given to individuals who made the biggest contribution to real system or organizational improvement. Another example concerns the then current CEO of the Yum!, David Novak, whom would give out $100 bills and plastic wind up chattering teeth, symbolic of putting a Yum on the customer's face, to recognize individuals during his visits to China.

However, one of the most powerful recognition programs we had at Yum! China was the national store operations team competition, called the CHAMPS Challenge. Store teams had to compete in operational competency from the area level up to the national level, with the winning team being recognized at the annual Store Managers Conference. It was quite an emotional experience for both the people attending the conference and the winners when they came up to receive their award.

People respond to recognition, so it is essential that you acknowledge your staff and develop programs that formalize recognition as part of your company's culture. This will help you achieve and maintain excellence.

Discipline with attention to detail and follow-up is important because it supports persistence and brings clarity. Maintaining discipline supports mental strength in striving for excellence. It also allows you to stay focused and on course as you work toward your desired outcome. In addition, discipline is critical for practice, and practice is what is needed if excellence is to be achieved.

The world-renowned violinist Itzhak Pearlman espouses the importance of practicing one's craft to reach excellence. In particular, he emphasizes practicing slowly and listening carefully in order to zero in on the details and make improvements accordingly. In Malcolm Gladwell's book *Outliers*, the author explains that the key to achieving excellence is to spend 10,000 hours on correct and expert practice. To do this, one must have the mental discipline to stay focused for hours at a time, and sometimes this means repeating a specific action, note, phrase or process repeatedly until it is just right.

Attention to detail impacts execution because without it, one will likely work sloppily or lack clarity. Think of the expression "The devil is in the details." It is no accident that the word "devil" is used here.

Follow-up is essential because excellence cannot be achieved without improvement, and improvement can only be made through correction. Follow-up will ensure that things are not left halfway done or just good enough. It will allow you to be vigilant as you monitor the implementation of your actions, and as you take corrective action on an as-needed basis. Following up also builds one's credibility, showing people they can count on you.

When it comes to follow-up, taking notes and jotting down to-do lists have worked wonders in my career. Nothing gets off the to-do list until it is done. In today's world of emails, it is also helpful to create a type of virtual "purgatory" in order to stay on track. What I do is create a folder in my email, and anything that needs action or follow-up goes into that folder. I review it on a weekly basis, but I access it daily and move things in and out as required. It is important, then, to make sure you set up your email folders correctly so that you can file each message properly for reference or action. And don't forget to use the delete function as appropriate to help keep things tidy. In short, don't let anything slip through the cracks, digital or otherwise.

Alignment ensures that different team members, departments and business units are moving in a coordinated manner toward the agreed-upon goals and objectives. Over the years, I have found that employees have a tendency, while toiling away, to become misaligned with one another and/or the objectives of the company. So, one of the roles of the leader is to ensure that people stay aligned.

The cornerstone in driving alignment is communication. People have to know what the objectives are, and they have to be updated periodically on where the company and their own performance stand in relation to those objectives. To do this, there should be formal and informal processes to ensure alignment. An example of a formal process is the employee performance review that takes place at six-month intervals. Another is the weekly staff meeting that a leader holds with his direct reports. An informal example is a chat with an employee near the water cooler, an opportunity the supervisor uses as a chance to align.

Lack of alignment between departments or people can be costly, because it often results in wasted time or effort. As a leader, I always think of who else should be informed about the status of a particular situation, and I will either cc: them on related email correspondence, include them in applicable meetings or take action in another relevant way. This may result in excessive communication at times, but that is better than a lack of alignment.

Mutual respect and empathy in communications are critical to ensuring healthy discord when necessary. All too often, interaction and communication are overly polite in the business world, and it's important not to confuse politeness with respect. Those who communicate in a polite manner use niceties, and they seldom say what they are really thinking in order to avoid offending others. This may, in fact, keep communication superficial. And while this type of communication is usually good for mingling at a cocktail party, it does not do much for building operational excellence because it is not deep enough.

Using a communication style that has respect at its core is an effective way of driving excellence because it allows one to offer deeper and more substantive feedback, even though it may bring about uncomfortable feelings in the person who is on the receiving end. The key is to communicate in a way where all parties can maintain their dignity, and in a way that doesn't come off as a personal attack. In order to accomplish this, the communication must be respectful and empathetic. What I mean by using empathy in communication, is putting yourself in the other person's shoes and imagining how you would feel if you were to hear what you are about to say. Empathy will help make you a more effective communicator because people will be more receptive to your feedback. Moreover, it will make you a better leader, allowing you to get more out of your people and drive better outcomes because it demonstrates respect which in turn supports trust.

Here is a scenario that demonstrates how politeness can interfere with driving operational excellence. At a company staff meeting, the Head of Finance presented a number of areas where it seemed that operating costs were misaligned and the Head of Finance went on to offer suggestions on how to address the issues. The Head of Operations, in turn, listened to the presentation, and while he harbored concerns about the suggestions, he decided it was better to be polite at the meeting than to confront the Head of Finance. He merely thanked his colleague and said that he would take a look at the suggestions and consider them. What happened afterward was that since the Head of Operations had some concerns and wanted to remain polite, he decided to avoid conflict above all else, and he employed a host of tactics to stall any further discussion.

Had the Head of Operations employed a communication style based on mutual respect, he would not have been concerned about politeness. After the presentation, he would have thanked his colleague for his insights and voiced that he had a few concerns about some of the suggestions, which he would have briefly explained. On the spot, he would have arranged a time to meet with the Head of Finance to follow up on the action steps. The difference between these two approaches is that the mutual respect approach enabled direct and open dialogue, which led to a follow-up meeting and real improvement. Both parties, while not in full agreement, were able to work together quickly to drive outcomes because they were not engaged in a charade of politeness.

Differences of opinion and disagreement are important and natural in a company and among people, but improvement depends on the reflection and discourse associated with this disagreement. If there is a culture that fosters trust and respect, communication should be more productive and serve to drive excellence. Say what must be said, be truthful yet respectful, and be empathetic.

The Outer Ring - Tools, Processes, Measurement, Feedback and Communication

The outer ring of the operations excellence model consists of a number of tools and processes that work in unison to drive operational excellence. It's important to keep in mind that these have the highest rate of success when used to mutually reinforce the steps one must take to achieve excellence. The tools and processes of the outer ring fall into the following categories: *planning, communication, audits, people management and development.*

This chapter will discuss each of these in greater detail, but it is important to note that the introduction or use of these without the core, as discussed in the preceding chapters, would be akin to buying a new, state-of-the-art golf club without having perfected your swing or concentration, and then expecting the club to help lower your handicap.

Planning for operational excellence typically starts in an unconscious manner, with the founder(s) walking the talk and striving for excellence. They tend to hire like-minded, capable people. Initially, this will suffice to get things moving, but it will stall once the company starts to scale up, because the founder's influence will have spread too thin. Also, this will not serve the company in a sustainable manner – not to long-term operational excellence – especially once the founder has moved on, because "the how" has not been codified and institutionalized. So, if you are a leader of a startup that is just getting off the ground, it's critical that you plan for the future and take sufficient time to spell out the company's mission statement. Commit the company's core values to writing.

In the case of an existing company, where there is already a culture and perhaps existing tools and processes in place, it is imperative that an assessment be made to see what adjustments are needed and what gaps there are that may be causing the organization to miss its operational excellence benchmarks. The key here, though, is for the leader to have an idea or vision of what these benchmarks should be. Then leaders must plan for how and when to make the changes.

At the core of this planning process is gaining clarity on what a company stands for and what it values, what its mission is and how leaders want team members to conduct themselves. The point is to bring clarity to the company culture so it will manifest in the mission and core value statements.

It is beyond the scope of this book to delve into detail on how to write a company mission and value statement, so I suggest that the reader refer to the following books for additional knowledge: *The Mission Statement Book* by Jeffrey Abrahams and *115 Mission Statements and Core Values: plus How to Write a Mission Statement that Works* by T. Calla and A. Cherry.

What I will say is that a company's mission statement can be changed as frequently as necessary. This is often done as new businesses are acquired and sold, or as the marketplace and technology change. But a company's values and statement thereof are enduring and underpin the mission statement. These values state with clarity, in a succinct manner, which qualities are important to the company and can apply universally to the different businesses the company may own.

For example, a value statement could say that the organization treats its customers, business partners and employees with respect. Yum! China actually had something similar to that. And the truth is that this same value can just as easily apply to a company that makes airplanes.

To use General Electric's 2014 Annual Report as an example, the company expressed its core beliefs as follows: "1. Customers determine our success. This is a statement of fact. Great teams win in the market. 2. Stay lean to go fast. Scarcity drives teamwork, will and accountability. 3. Learn and adapt to win. Good companies make mistakes quickly, but they learn and adjust. And, winning has to be our goal. 4. Empower and inspire each other. The days of centralized command are in the past. Our teams have the expertise to accept empowerment and drive results. 5. Deliver results in an uncertain world. This is our commitment to you. GE Beliefs drive performance and shape careers."

This is a perfect example of a set of values or beliefs that are equally applicable to a range of companies, from those that make airplanes to those that design software. These beliefs shape how the employees perform their jobs and interact with one another, which has direct impact on the quality of their outcomes. It also enables flexibility, because these values apply to everything the company does today or tomorrow.

After I assumed the role of Chief Operating Officer in the company that had franchise and the development rights for the sandwich brand Subway in Shanghai, I worked with the founder to review the company's value statement. It had all of the essential and ethical elements – except one. It turned out the value statement failed to address excellence in execution. That isn't to say these elements weren't present in the company culture, but they weren't explicitly stated. Thus, people weren't consciously focused on in the way they needed to be to drive operational outcomes. In this case, I was fortunate that the values were solid and needed only one clarification. Had it been that the values were substantially lacking, the situation would have demanded more drastic measures, and not all organizations can withstand that type of change. I also had experience with what can happen when a company fails to adapt to necessary changes in its culture, and it's not a pretty picture as it tore things apart.

The budget and planning process is where narrative and the numbers reconcile. It usually takes the form of spreadsheets, where cash flow projection is the key, and it also requires presentations to explain the underlying assumptions, numbers, strategy and tactics.

For large companies with a lot of resources, this can be quite an involved process but I believe that even a small owner-operator business should use this as an opportunity to drive outcomes.

Early in my career, I learned an effective planning and brainstorming tool from my boss at the time – who was General Manager of American Life Insurance Company in Taipei – and I still use this method today. It's called *mind mapping*, and if you want a quick introduction on this subject, an excellent resource is *Mind Mapping for Dummies* by Florian Rustler. But I will say here that the general idea behind mind mapping is that the mind, in its creative state, does not go about its business in a linear fashion. Also, pictures and symbols help harness the creative power of the mind. The tool enables one to capture quickly related branches of ideas and thoughts as they are formed. For a simple planning project, this could be done on the back of a napkin, but bigger paper is needed for more complicated projects, for example, I've even made very large mind maps on poster board over the years. Once the mind map is complete, it is then transposed to a linear list or PowerPoint to add detail to the framework. I actually started the writing of this book with a mind map.

The budget and planning process is critical to driving operational excellence because this is where a winning strategy is hammered out. It is also what provides focus and direction for the entire organization, from the shareholders down to part-time or casual workers. It quantifies expectations, which in turn supports accountability, enabling measurement and auditing as well.

From a buy-in standpoint, it is also important that the planning process be as inclusive as possible and this ties into the section on accountability. If people feel they have input and are included, it is more likely they will have ownership and demonstrate accountably.

Once the objectives, strategy, plan and budget are set, it's critical that all parts of the organization are in alignment, and that people get "on fire" to strive for completion. By "on fire" I mean getting people motivated and passionate about what's at hand.

One method to help get people "on fire" is to pay special attention to how the objectives are communicated and supported. Highlighting one or two of the key objectives is more effective than having a list serve as the organization's rallying cry. Then, these highlighted objectives need to permeate throughout the organization in such processes as employee incentives, departmental and personal objectives, and performance reviews.

The objectives and rallying cries have to be worded in simple and powerful terms, making use of symbols or images whenever possible. The objective is to make it clear, easy to remember, and emotionally enabling to get people "on fire" to drive outcomes. For example, for a retail chain with 263 existing stores, and with a budget target of opening 37 new stores in the coming fiscal year, one way to state the objective would be "To open 37 new stores in 2016," but a more inspiring way to state it would be "300 in 2016!" The focus is on the big number, and it is easy to remember. To extrapolate, "300 in 2016!" can be used as a motivational chant at meetings and gatherings throughout the year. Also, the number 300 is visually appealing, and posters where the number 300 is embellished can be placed strategically throughout the office. The zeros, for example, can be modified as smiley faces, connoting the satisfaction that will come when the 300-store count objective is reached. This is a way to get the whole organization behind the objectives and involved in driving outcomes.

Auditing and measuring for operational excellence involves setting standards and measuring performance against those standards. It also entails taking corrective action, making adjustments as needed and re-measuring. Available tools include checklists and audits, mystery shops, people performance processes, business reviews, meetings and functions.

Through practice, athletes make this a major part of what they do. However, they don't engage in mindless practice, so to be effective, it must be done with purpose, often focusing on a particular aspect of the game or on a specific skill. Also, it is usually done under the watchful eye of a coach.

Even if a skill has been perfected, bad habits can sneak in and throw an athlete off. Golf pro Tiger Woods had regular coaching on his game, and he switched coaches on a regular basis – even after winning various world titles. Businesses are no different, and execution needs to be practiced, measured and coached.

One of the most basic tools companies can use to measure execution is the audit. Many people think of tax or accounting when they hear the word audit, but I am referring to an operational audit. And the key to driving excellence with an operational audit is to properly identify what it is you should be auditing, what benchmarks you are using and how you will measure them.

The starting point for measuring is determining how you will measure and what you will measure against. In terms of driving operational excellence, execution has to be measured against a specific set of standards. And these standards need to be set in a manner that will drive people to reach for excellence.

Note that there is a difference between standards and expectations. For example, when measuring operational excellence in customer service, it may be tempting to look at how well the company delivers against customers' expectations. I would argue, though, that a more accurate way of going about this is to measure how the company is executing against its own standards. Expectations can be hard to manage because they deal more with perception, whereas execution against standards is more clear-cut. I don't mean that customer expectations are unimportant. Indeed, it is critical that company standards be aligned with customer expectations from the beginning, and evaluated on a regular basis to ensure they are still relevant.

Measuring execution and operational excellence against a specific set of standards will ensure that focus is put on performance and any gaps there might be. The underlying idea here is that standards have to be approved by the company. It should also mean that the company understands customer expectations, and that executives have developed the standards for their products and services that allow the company to deliver those products and services in a profitable and achievable manner.

As I mentioned, market research should be done to ascertain what customer expectations are and there are various techniques to do so, all of which fall into one of two broad groups: qualitative research, which entails focus groups; and quantitative research, which involves more reliance on data ascertained via questionnaires and data analysis. Such research can help guide strategy and set or adjust current standards. This research can also clarify how a company is executing against customer expectations, but internal auditing should still measure execution against company standards.

This perspective of measuring against standards will have a direct impact on how the various audit checklists and auditing tools are constructed. Here are some examples of how to word questions in an internal operations audit for a retail restaurant business.

Weak: Were customers greeted?
Strong: Were customers greeted with a smile and eye contact within 10 seconds of entering the store?

Note that 10 seconds is the standard greeting time, as described in the operations manual. Based on customer research, 10 seconds was determined as the most effective greeting time after a customer has entered the store.

Weak: Was the sandwich toasted to the customer's liking?
Strong: Was the sandwich toasted in the oven for 2 minutes in line with company standards?
Note: After extensive product and customer research, company leaders found that 2 minutes in the oven was the optimal time to toast a sandwich and deliver an experience that will please the typical customer.

A Mystery Shopper is a person who is hired by the company, usually through a third party, to pose as a customer and report on the experience. The individual observations are consolidated and compiled by the third-party vendor into a report, which is then submitted to management. There are companies that specialize in this type of market intelligence, and some consulting or marketing companies can also provide this service.

It is also a form of audit, but the angle of approach is more from the customer's perspective, whereas an operations audit is from an internal perspective. There may very well be gaps between the outcomes of the two, but the goal should be to narrow those gaps. High scores on both ends indicate that employees are executing consistently against the standards. And if those standards are set correctly, you are driving operational excellence and customer satisfaction.

The best programs I have found are ongoing in which the results have consequences. To optimize the effectiveness of these programs, results must be integrated with the people performance processes discussed later in this chapter. For example, the results should be integrated with employee bonuses and performance reviews.

Yum! China had a very effective mystery shop program called CHAMPS, which involved real customers reporting their experiences at the stores. The operations team reviewed the results on a monthly basis, and the entire program was integrated into the operations team's people performance review process. The goal was always to reach 100% on CHAMPS, and the few stores that were able to get twelve consecutive months of 100% earned some very special recognition.

With the Subway sandwich brand I managed at another company, we also made very effective use of a third-party mystery shop program in Shanghai. In combination with other initiatives, we were able to drive a measurable twenty-point operational improvement in our mystery shop scores over a fifteen-month period. This led to very positive consequences on sales and the bottom line.

The design of the mystery shop audit or checklist must follow the same guidelines mentioned previously about audit design, but measure and evaluate it from the customer's perspective. For example, in the case of Subway, we had questions such as, "Were you greeted upon entering the store within 10 seconds?" and "Were you asked if you wanted "double meat" or "double cheese" on your sandwich when you placed your order?" In the case of the second example, ensuring that each customer is asked if they wanted extra meat or cheese drives profitability, because there is an extra charge for these items, and in many cases, customers will say yes. This means incremental revenue. It follows the well-known and proven practice at McDonald's, where they ask, "Do you want fries with that?" In the end, it's a numbers game.

You do not have to operate a retail or restaurant company to make use of a mystery shop program. It may require a bit more creativity to structure a program where the mystery shopper can remain anonymous though but it can be done. A company can also contact customers about their recent experience directly, but this is different than mystery shopping and more akin to research. For example, I often receive surveys via email after hotel stays or airline flights. Surely this type of feedback can be useful and ultimately help drive operational excellence as well especially when combined with a mystery shop program.

The other aspect of a mystery shop program is the randomness of it. The employees know about the program, and they should be fully aware of what they are being measured on. In other words, know what the mystery shoppers are looking at and expecting which should be exactly what the customers are looking for. The program helps ensure precise execution because employees know the rewards for an outstanding review and the consequences of a poor one, yet they do not know when they will be audited by a mystery shopper.

People management and development tools and processes support the people-centric core of the operational excellence model. This component gains substance by the use of:

1. Committees;
2. A people performance review system that includes job descriptions, objectives and employee performance reviews, or 360 feedback;
3. Bench-planning;
4. Various training courses with manuals;
5. A mentor program, as discussed in the chapter on The Core – The Right Culture;
6. Coaching, which was also discussed in the chapter entitled "The Core – The Right Culture";
7. Recognition and incentive programs;
8. Delegation;
9. Meetings, reviews and functions.

Before I explain more about each of these aspects, I would like to reinforce a point about "know-how." Professionals, through formal training and experience, accumulate know-how.

Consequently, know-how is more than just knowledge, as it encompasses understanding, which has at its root, experience. This know-how is what helps a company make effective decisions and drive strategy and profitability. There is a unique book that elaborates further on the subject, entitled *Business Beyond the Box: Applying Your Mind for Breakthrough Results* by John O'Keeffe. Yum! China actually had an internal training course with the very same title, which was actually based on this book.

1) Committees: It's important for the long-term sustainability of a company that this know-how is shared and passed on to more junior executives and employees within the company. This can be accomplished through training courses and manuals, but another effective way is through the use of decision-making committees. These committees are typically composed of cross-functional leaders who offer differing perspectives and fields of expertise, enabling the company to accumulate know-how.

Yum! China made very effective use of expert committees, with the objective of making better decisions by leveraging cross-functional know-how and perspective, and by developing junior executives. There were various committees, such as the Margin Management Committee and the New Product Committee, and even the Real Estate Committee. As head of the Franchise Development Department, I was the Chairman of the Franchise Committee. The role of the Committee was to set franchise policy and approve franchise candidates. The committee was made up of four primary voting members and four backup members for interviewing, who came from various functions, such as operations, finance and marketing. No one dominated the discussions, and there was never gridlock. There was consensus-building on policy, and decisions were usually made – and perspectives shared – at the end of each meeting. I have established similar decision committees at subsequent companies with great effect and find this a very effective way to manage.

2) The people performance review is a critical tool to drive operational excellence because it enables effective management of a company's key resource – its people.

The process begins by hiring the right people, which we have discussed this in the previous chapter. However, before starting the interview and recruiting process, it's essential to have proper and well-thought-out job descriptions that tie into the organizational chart.

It is amazing how many companies I have worked for and interviewed at that either don't have job descriptions or have job descriptions that are outdated or incomplete. Also, many of the job descriptions I have seen simply list out the duties that the candidate is expected to execute, but omit one critical aspect – that is, the behaviors that the candidate is expected to demonstrate. Naturally, these behaviors must be in line with the company culture and values, as we discussed in the first chapter of the book.

For example, one item on the job description for a Franchise Director, a task-oriented role, may be, "Recruit qualified franchise candidates in line with annual budgets." But the same item reworked to include a behavioral aspect is, "Recruit qualified franchise candidates in line with annual budgets and in a manner consistent with the company's core values." If one of the company's core values is to treat colleagues, suppliers and customers with respect, and in a manner that you yourself would like to be treated, then by including this in the job description you are further reinforcing the company culture and driving this value into daily execution. Similarly, as further reinforcement, I like to include the following in my job descriptions: "Walk the talk of the company values in all you do." After all, everyone in the company is a brand ambassador.

As mentioned, the job description should be more than a listing of duties and expectations. It also lays the foundation for annual personal objectives, which are established in line with budget goals. To really drive down the process, these personal objectives must be formally integrated into an annual review sub-process, as discussed below.

Objective setting will drive operational excellence because it is the basis of measuring performance and coaching opportunities. And if objectives are properly aligned with the overall annual budget and strategy, they serve to drive down on a granular and relevant basis, function by function, department by department, and employee by employee, the macro objectives of the company. In other words, they provide focus.

There are many books and techniques to use for objective setting, but I have found the **S.M.A.R.T.** method to be both simple and effective. This is an acronym to help formulate objectives, and it stands for *Specific, Measureable, Achievable, Relevant and Time-bound.* My general experience with employees who are not familiar with this technique is that objectives tend to be too vague and difficult to measure. A great book to learn more about this subject is *S.M.A.R.T. Goals Made Simple: 10 Steps to Master Your Personal and Career Goals* by S.J. Scott.

An example of a S.M.A.R.T. objective for a store manager of a retail food outlet could be, "to increase year on year beverage sales at my store by 5% while maintaining overall beverage margin during the high season between April 1st and September 10th." The reader will notice that it is specific, zeroing in on one product category – beverages. It is measureable, as it spells out that it is comparing year on year results, and the objective states exactly what the increase needs to be (5%). This objective is also achievable because beverage sales for the preceding year over the same period were flat, and the preceding year also experienced unseasonal rainy weather, which negatively impacted beverage sales. As such, the Manager believes that such weather is unlikely to occur again this year, and she has an aggressive operations and marketing plan in mind. This is a relevant objective, because increasing profit is what the shareholders and her boss are looking for, and they have specifically mentioned beverage sales as an opportunity in the annual budget.

It is noteworthy to mention that that the Manger included wording in her objective that shows her understanding that it is possible to drive up beverage sales through discounting so she added wording that requires her to maintain the current margin. She has also adequately covered the criteria of being time-bound by spelling out a specific period to achieve the results, from April 1st through September 10th.

To integrate objectives with performance, the objectives must form the cornerstone of the performance review template. I have used a format that separates objectives into two groups. Group one covers the example above, and it is focuses on hard core tasks and objectives. The second group consists of personal and professional developmental objectives, with the intention of motivating and developing the employee so that he or she can make even greater contributions to the company in the long-term. Over the years, I have had employees include such things as improving their proficiency at reading financial statements and honing their English and communications skills, and they have met these objectives by attending seminars, completing training courses and reading books. These address broader skill gaps they had that and if improved, would help them contribute more to the company in the long-term, making them more promotable in the process. Employees will also become more well-rounded and able to take on additional responsibility.

Once effective job descriptions have been written, and the right people recruited and objectives set, employees need to be coached in both a formal and informal manner. Performance and 360-degree reviews are formal methods of providing feedback to employees. 360-degree reviews are usually done by a third-party agency. What happens is that the outside firm gives a standard form to a sample group of an employee's customers, colleagues supervisor, and subordinates, so that person can be evaluated and receive confidential and anonymous feedback. It's anonymous because the person being evaluated won't be told who gave what feedback. There is some controversy over the effectiveness of 360-degree reviews, but I have participated in a number of them over the course of my career, and I've found them helpful – especially in identifying blind spots. Blind spots in performance are behaviors you are exhibiting – things you are either doing or not doing – that you were not aware of, and that you'll find out about from the feedback.

Often, if these are not properly addressed, they can derail your career.

Performance reviews are also done with a set form, usually the very form that was used to set your objectives at the beginning of the year. I usually have my team first fill out their review, and then I do one myself. Afterward, we meet to compare the two. This is an excellent way of identifying any blind spots or misalignment issues.

As a supervisor and a coach, it's imperative to provide specific and concrete feedback, and to include examples whenever possible. In this way, there will be no ambiguity, and the employee will know exactly what to work on.

The performance review serves as a tool to help employees grow, perfect and improve their overall performance and skills. And for those who can't or won't respond to the feedback, the performance review becomes a tool to manage them out of the organization. I have found that there are situations where certain people are simply not coachable. More often than not, the root of this lies in the attitude of the employee.

There is a very effective tool I learned many years ago, from a colleague, that I have used with great effect to gain clarity on who will focus on development and coaching efforts and who will not respond to coaching. It's called the *Can & Can't / Will & Won't Matrix.*

Here's how it works. Take a rectangular box and split it into quadrants, with the upper left quadrant labeled "Can" and the upper right quadrant labeled "Can't." Starting at the upper left of the box is the label "Will," and below that, next to the bottom left quadrant, is the label "Won't." Labeling in this manner allows the matrix to represent the interaction of skills and attitudes, and how they influence a person's development potential. The "Can and Can't" category refers to a person's hard core, functional and managerial capability, as in whether or not they can they do the job. "Will and Won't," in turn, refers to their attitude, or whether or not they want to do the job.

The objective is to write the names of the people on your team in the appropriate quadrants, as you have determined they fit based on their use of the tools and procedures from the people development process. Over time, you want to get all of your people into the upper left corner, where they are both capable and willing ("Can & Will"). For people that fall into the "Can't & Won't" and "Can & Won't" quadrants, a team leader must evaluate if the attitude issues can be dealt with quickly.

I believe that no matter how much training you provide, if employees do not have the right attitude, you will always be dealing with subpar performance. So, determine if you can move these people into the "Can't & Will" or "Can & Will" quadrants in a timely fashion. If not, they probably need to be managed out of the company. You, as a leader, should spend a significant amount of your development time on the people in the "Can't and Will" quadrant, with the objective of getting them into the "Can and Will" quadrant; that's what will drive operational excellence.

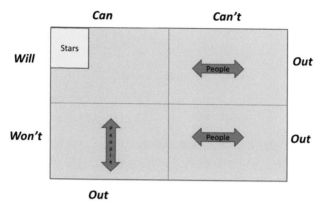

Can & Can't / Will & Won't Matrix

It's not easy to be on the receiving end of a performance review, so it's important to keep an open mind when you listen to feedback, and to honestly evaluate what is being said. Early on in my career at Blockbuster, I received some excellent coaching from one of our international Directors of Human Resources. He said that when you hear feedback, take it all on board. It may be that you only have control over, let's say, forty percent of the issues expressed in the feedback, and it may be that you only agree with thirty percent that. But that thirty percent is a great place to begin making changes. In other words, focus on what you have control over, what you know to be true and begin immediately. You will be a better professional for it, and certainly a lot less stressed, as you will no longer focus on what you cannot control. His advice to me was invaluable, and it changed my career for the better.

As a supervisor, when writing performance reviews and giving feedback, it's important to have the mindset that you are providing this feedback in order to coach and help your employees become better professionals and execute their jobs more effectively. You have to be honest and direct, but always act with empathy and respect. Imagine how you would feel receiving the feedback you are about to give, and word it appropriately. Nonetheless, keep in mind that what has to be said must be said.

Ideally, though, you have developed a relationship of trust with your employee, so they will most likely understand your positive intentions and be receptive to the feedback. If the reader wants to better understand how trust plays a role in everything we do, please refer to the book *The SPEED of TRUST: The One Thing That*

Changes Everything by Stephen M .R. Covey with Rebecca R. Merrill.

In terms of timing, coaching is provided on an as-needed basis, but I have found that it is effective to conduct the formal performance review midyear, and then again at the end of the year. If you are coaching your employees on a regular basis, there should be no major surprises come review time. The formal review forces both parties to reflect and express their feedback in writing. Writing it down especially helps with clarity and alignment, and it provides a record for future reference.

3) The term "bench strength" is taken from its meaning in sports. The term is a reference to having enough quality players to substitute should a key player be injured or in need of rest. In business, the term has come to mean having enough in-house talent to fill leadership positions as they become available. While candidates can always be recruited externally, it is motivating to have the option to promote internally. There are other benefits to this as well. For example, internal candidates are already acclimatized to the operating environment and company culture, and they have existing relationships

with personnel and an understanding of the business. This usually translates to a very short ramp-up period. The downside to only using internal candidates, however, is that it's like inbreeding, and in today's fast-moving business world, it is important to get outside perspectives and experience in order to stay fresh and challenge the establishment. Consequently, I am an advocate for a mix of internal promotions and external recruitment.

My first encounter with formal bench-planning was at Blockbuster Taiwan. I was Director of Operations at the time, and we had ninety company-run stores all over the island. As in any retail business, turnover was a concern, especially at the Store Manager level. So, we had to ensure we had adequate bench strength to replace departing Store Managers and hire appropriately for any new stores we opened. My second encounter with a formal bench-planning process was at Yum! China and it was directed at head office management staff to plan for the continued development and growing complexity of the business.

In both cases, it entailed using the processes mentioned in this book: performance reviews, 360's, audit results and more to identify performers and employees who exhibited development potential. Then, these candidates were exposed to training and mentoring programs. In the case of Yum! China, this sometimes involves departmental rotation.

At Blockbuster Taiwan, we had to ascertain which Assistant Managers were ready for promotion to Store Manager, and in what timeframe (i.e., six, eight or twelve months). Then, we had to identify the gaps in each person's skills. Subsequently, we were able to put them through a combination of formal and informal training and coaching to get them up to speed and ensure we had people ready to take on more responsibility when we needed it.

In order to drive operational excellence, an organization needs to ensure it has capable people. Besides recruiting externally, there needs to be a program to evaluate and develop internal candidates to take on bigger roles before the need actually arises.

4) In addition to coaching and mentoring, there must be a formal training process in place to help develop employees and ensure that there is adequate bench strength. I have found that there are two general types of training: that which focuses on soft skills and culture and that which focuses on hard, functional skills. The latter often involves a component of on-the-job training. In my various leadership roles, I had the Human Resources department lead the development and rollout of the former, with function heads and Human Resources developing and disseminating the second type of training.

The soft skills and culture training includes subjects like leadership, decision-making, service, teamwork and more. At Yum! China, we had a number of courses such as "Business Beyond the Box," which were required for head office managerial employees and other higher-ups. One of the most useful training sessions I ever had was at Blockbuster Video Australia. The Human Resources department organized an outside consulting company to come in and conduct the Myers-Briggs personality test, complete with training on how to interpret the results. By the end of the session, we had a better understanding of our personal management and communication styles and what that meant. What I learned that day has stayed with me throughout my career.

The hard, functional training is all about what one needs to skillfully carry out a specific job. And this typically relies heavily on the use of operations manuals, job aids, regulation guides and training videos. Restaurant chains of all types have very detailed operations manuals, which explain everything from how to clean equipment to how to handle food. It is not enough to have an employee simply read the manuals; there is usually a component of on-the-job training where the student has to demonstrate functional competency. In the above example, it is usually the operations training department that leads the training, but the Human Resources department can act as a source of checks and balances by auditing the implementation of the program. Operational excellence has to be driven by effective training, which covers both the soft and hard aspects that are required of employees.

5) Mentoring was discussed in the second chapter of the book, "The Core – The Right Culture."

6) Coaching was also discussed in the second chapter, "The Core – The Right Culture."

7) There are many ways of designing incentive and bonus schemes, and one size does not fit all. One thing to keep in mind, however, is that all schemes and plans are meant to incentivize, so they must make it worth the effort, and the objectives must be set high enough to make a real difference for the business but they must be achievable.

Besides having an annual incentive scheme, especially for operations or sales-focused teams, utilizing shorter incentive evaluation periods can be an effective way to drive outcomes toward the annual goal. Often, incentive schemes are drawn up to focus on the numbers. Did the company, division or unit hit its target sales, growth or EBITDA numbers? This is important, but there is more to it than that, and the secret to driving operational excellence is to link culture and performance with the incentive. For example, it is important to look beyond the sales, costs, growth or cash flow numbers; the truth is that audit and mystery shop scores should be linked to the incentives. The idea here is that if the employees are driving audit and mystery shop scores, they should be driving sales and brand equity as well. Effective incentives, coupled with an integrated recognition program, work extremely well to drive excellence and outcomes, getting people "on fire" and keeping them motivated.

8) One very effective way to develop employees is to ensure that they are properly engaged through delegation. Delegation is the assignment of tasks and projects that go beyond the day to-day responsibilities of the employee. These tasks and projects can be part of something bigger, something that affects the whole department, brand or even the company. It is very inspiring and engaging for most professionals to know that they are working on something that really makes a difference, even if it is only one piece of that bigger pie. It also builds teamwork by allowing people to contribute to something greater. Often, the very act of delegation shows the employee that the

leader has confidence in them, and this display of confidence is in itself motivational.

People have different work styles and ambitions, so leaders must be sensitive to the level of responsibility they delegate to ensure the employee doesn't shut down from overload or become unmotivated from lack of stimulation. A lack of delegation can be quite tragic, because it indicates that the leader is missing out on two very important opportunities. One, the opportunity to get the best out of their people through the motivational power of delegation, and from the corresponding learning and growth; and two, the professional freedom they themselves experience by having more time to focus on bigger, more forward-looking issues that will continue to create shareholder value.

Done the right way, delegation drives operational excellence through employee engagement, professional growth and motivation.

9) Business reviews, meetings and functions are all powerful ways to drive operational excellence because they align and motivate.

1) Business reviews, in order to be effective, need to be properly structured and held on a regular basis. Business is moving faster than ever in today's world because of the speedy flow of information, which is driven especially by mobile technology and social media. As a result, I believe that senior executives have to delegate more and empower their people to make quicker decisions, but this can't happen in a vacuum, and this is where the business review can help. Not only does it serve to keep the team informed and aligned, but it provides a mechanism to monitor results, give feedback and coach.

Typically, this type of review is done on a monthly basis, and the process is one where subordinates present the results for the reporting period in a formal manner. The format is first set and it requires reporting on operational Key Performance Indicators (KPIs) that tie into many of the topics in this book. For example, if the company has a mystery shop program and an operational audit program, the scores with action items should be reported during the business review process. In this way, attendees can quickly gauge performance against benchmarks. Attendees of these reviews should include their line manager, department or business head and same-level members of their team; and other cross-functional staff members as appropriate. This may include a finance department representative who can provide additional perspective and improve his or her operational understanding and alignment from the review. For example, if you are a District Manager at a retail or sales company, other District Managers will attend the review, as well as your supervisor, who could be the Director of Operations.

2) Meetings are effective because of their frequency and intimacy. For example, the classic "staff meeting" is usually held on a weekly basis, and the leader typically has his direct reports participate in the meeting. It can be in-

person, a video meeting or a teleconference, and the agenda often includes topics such as updates, sales performance, sales trends for the current week, etc. There is no specific formula for this type of meeting, and the agenda will vary based on the industry, team size and company priorities. However, there are a few points to keep in mind that I believe are important to ensure that these meetings help drive operational excellence.

Meetings need to be time-constrained in order to foster focus. I have experienced, and been responsible for time overrun in many meetings, and I have reflected heavily on this. In my opinion, for a typical staff meeting, the ideal time constraint should be sixty to ninety minutes. To achieve this, one must take further discussion of certain issues that surface during the meeting "offline." That is, one must set up a separate meeting with the relevant parties to discuss the issue further, rather than wasting the time of the people who are present but not involved. I have found that this issue is the major cause of time overrun in meetings.

Meetings need to have a set agenda and format that focuses on the key operational metrics and issues at hand. For example, discuss sales for the reporting week vs. budget, and the reasons for any positive or negative variances. Then have a discussion on a forecast of the current week's sales and what the outcome is likely to be. Again, include a discussion on projected variances. If there are any special issues that need to be discussed, it is a good idea to provide advance notice so these items can be added to the agenda. At staff meetings, a common practice is to "go around the table" and allow attendees to give a quick update on their own issues. This can be helpful for alignment, but personnel should avoid using the staff meeting as a substitute for what should in fact be one-on-one discussions. In addition, it is best that these meetings remain apolitical. I have seen situations where tension exists between employees, and they do not wish to engage directly, so they use the staff meeting as a public venue to resolve the issue. A leader cannot allow this to happen.

Taking meeting minutes is very important because it is effective to have a record of what was discussed, especially to keep track of any decisions that were made or any issues that require follow-up. For example, suppose it was decided that a separate meeting should be set up to discuss product quality issues. By including this in the staff meeting minutes, there will be no excuse to allow this additional meeting to slip through the cracks and not take place.

Whenever possible, recognition should be given at these meetings to reinforce the core of the operational excellence model – culture. It can be from one team member to another for outstanding support, or from the leader to a team member so that the team leaves the meeting better aligned, informed, clearer, and more motivated to drive operational outcomes.

3) Company functions include events such as teambuilding, annual manager meetings and dinners. These drive operational excellence because they support the core of the model; namely, culture. These functions are even more important in today's business environment because more people than ever are working remotely due to technology. As such, fewer team members get their daily dose of cultural reinforcement by coming into the office each day, and having the opportunity to develop relationships around the water cooler has become a less available.

I have participated in, and organized many functions over the years, at various companies, and I firmly believe that as a leader, they are indispensable in driving alignment, direction and reinforcement of the company culture. In addition, they are extremely motivational, not to mention a great platform for teambuilding and development. As a participant, I have found them usually informative, always helpful in reinforcing relationships and sometimes stimulating.

Teambuilding activities include group problem-solving activities such as a mystery escape, where groups work together to solve a series of mysteries and puzzles in order to escape from a room. Another variation are activities where, under a fixed amount of time, teams have to build a structure with the provided supplies, and a competition ensues for the most creative, durable and effective structure. Paintball is another effective and fun activity I have participated in. In this case, employees are split into teams, and they have to communicate and strategize to beat the other teams during a game of paintball.

These structured activities usually have the purpose of highlighting the importance of communication and teamwork while being done in a fun way.

An example of a people development and alignment function is where the event begins with a top-level year-end summary (or a summary of year-to-date performance). This can include sales growth, number of stores opened, products developed, etc. Then, senior leadership can give a broad overview of the operating plan and what lies ahead for the following year. Once this is done, the next item on the agenda can be developmental. It can take the form of having a guest speaker come to talk about a related motivational topic or an executive conducting an in-house training course. Sometimes even having an external trainer teach a course on a given subject is effective.

Over the years, not only have I been in companies where senior leadership used all of these approaches to drive outcomes and operational excellence, but I did so myself at the companies I led. For example, at Blockbuster Taiwan, where I was Director of Operations, we wanted to develop a more customer-centric culture among our Store Managers, and at one meeting we had an outside consultant come in and conduct a course on customer service, what it was and how we could apply it to our brand. I worked closely with the consultant to develop the material so that it was relevant to the issues at hand. Our Human Resources department was also involved; they actually found the consultant and helped coordinate the event.

These functions are also a great way to drive recognition in a public forum, as it is extremely powerful to recognize achievement in front of one's peers. Examples include recognition for the top sales manager, or for the store with the highest operational improvement, or even for an employee who has demonstrated outstanding service.

Very often, these functions include a lunch or dinner, and depending on the company culture, there may be entertainment during the meals. As the Franchise Development Director at Yum! China, I organized a separate meeting for our Franchisees when they attended our annual Store Manager conference. And I always tried to include a dinner with live entertainment, great food and plenty of drink; especially alcohol. One year, we had our meeting in Inner Mongolia and as a team activity, we went horseback riding during the day, and in the evening we had a dinner featuring local dishes, including a whole spitted lamb, and saw a performance by a traditional Mongolian dance troupe. It was a great teambuilding and bonding opportunity for our franchisees, especially with the free flow of the Chinese high-alcohol content drink called *Bai Jiu*.

During my time in Australia with Blockbuster Video, where I was the Franchise Business Consultant in Queensland, our franchisees were big golf players. As such, our meetings usually included golf as the teambuilding activity.

While the actual activities, cuisine, agenda or venue may differ based on the issues at hand, on the participant's preferences, and on the company and local culture, the basic principles of using functions to drive operational excellence is universal.

Communication is the lubricant that greases the entire operations excellence model and ensures that all parts interact smoothly. Communication entails the transfer of ideas and information, and effective communication, or the lack of it, can bind people together or drive them apart. This is an important subject, and it would take an entire book to give communication the credit it so deserves. If the reader wants to learn more, a quick starting point is to read *Communication Skills For Dummies* by Elizabeth Kuhnke. However, I would like to emphasize a few key points that I believe are critical in supporting operational excellence.

1) Communication is a two-way street, and it involves listening – not just talking. Regardless of who starts the discussion, the other party should not interrupt, but instead listen, no matter how high the emotional intensity of the conversation. Think of the last time you had a conversation with someone who kept interrupting you. I bet you felt frustrated, and I bet you agree that it was almost impossible to have a proper exchange of ideas. During an exchange, an excellent way to demonstrate that you have heard what the other person has said is to paraphrase what they told you. For example, you can say, "To make sure I heard you correctly, your concern is that you have been repeatedly unable to reach a customer service representative at our call center without waiting for fifteen minutes each time. Is that correct?"

To quote Steven Covey from his book *7 Habits of Highly Effective People*, (Habit 5) "Seek First to Understand, Then to be Understood" refers to listening with the intent of truly understanding the other person's point of view.

Besides interrupting others, another common habit that interferes with proper communication is inactive listening which occurs when the listener is not fully engaged because they are mentally preparing their response, or maybe they are seething about something that was just said. So, in order to foster effective communication, make it a habit to avoid interrupting others, and prioritize conscious listening in order to gain perspective on the other person's point of view. This will not only help you frame your own perspective and articulate it accordingly but will foster better communication.

2) As mentioned repeatedly in this book, alignment is critical, and it is especially so in today's fast-moving business world, where more people are working remotely. In general, over time, people will naturally become misaligned from one another and the company strategy or mission. This is often done unintentionally or unconsciously, as people focus on their day-to-day issues. So it is important to keep in mind that it is effective communication that will keep people stay aligned and focused. Imagine the analogy of a ship that gets taken off course due to wind and sea currents. The

captain and navigator have to work constantly and diligently to realign the ship and keep it on course. Well, the same thing applies to a business and its people.

3) Written communication is an area where I often see opportunities to improve alignment especially with the use of email, and more specifically, the use of "CC" and "BCC," which stands for *carbon copy* and *blind carbon copy*.

When discussing an issue via email, it is always good practice to think about who should be copied (CC) on the email, either because you need their assistance or because you believe they need the information to stay aligned. All too often, people are copied on emails for political reasons. For example, the author of an email may think, *I'm going to copy my boss on this email to cover myself, and also to ensure I get a response.* Certainly, email can be used in this manner, but in my opinion, this indicates a deeper issue related to execution or the company culture, and it is unlikely that these tactics will ensure long-term success at driving operational excellence, because too much energy will be expended on political shenanigans. The ultimate example of this is the use of BCC. I never use the BCC feature in my email practices, as I personally consider it unethical. This is because the person being written to has no idea there is a wider audience, and this can undermine the trust in your relationship if found out. Having said this, though, even when not using BCC, it is important to keep in mind that any email you send can and is likely to be read by someone other than the intended recipient, and that emails are usually stored on the company server in perpetuity. In other words, communicate and write responsibly. Make use of CC to keep people informed and aligned, and forget about the BCC function unless you send out a broadcast email and want to keep the recipients' email addresses confidential. Above all though, don't think of email as a substitute for face-to-face or verbal communication, because it is difficult to ascertain tone and expression in written communication, and misunderstandings can easily arise.

4) Operational excellence is also reliant on truth. By truth, I am referring to seeing and discussing things the way they really are.

There is a hint of Socratic methodology in what I am referring to, in that proper dialogue and questioning are used to gain clarity. However, note that being direct and honest doesn't mean being cruel, vulgar or rude. So, it is important to be clear and direct, but in a respectful and empathetic manner. I discussed empathy in communication in the first chapter of this book, which highlighted the importance of culture, the core of the operations excellence model.

In addition, proper word choice and communication highly influence clarity. Loose language often springs from lazy thought, and this can lead to misguided conclusions and incorrect action. Here is a loosely, poorly-thought-out statement from a subordinate to his supervisor as an example: "I have a feeling that the store's operations are substandard by the bad scores on recent checklists." The problem with this statement as it pertains to driving operational excellence is that it is not reliant on operational benchmarks and standards to provide a clear and accurate understanding. It would be more effective if the subordinate had said, "The store has scored below our operational benchmarks having received a 76% on its last operations audit and a 56% on its last mystery shop."

Communicating with clarity does not come naturally to many people, yet it needs to be part of the company culture. This means that it needs to be practiced and reinforced on a daily basis and supported with training and the company culture.

Tying It All Together

When looking to drive operational excellence, one needs to look first at the company culture. Adjust it if need be, and make sure the leaders walk the talk and lead by example.

Look then at the organizational structure and the people in it to determine if they are compatible with the culture and fit into the structure. One might find that a new organizational structure is needed to increase transparency and accountability so make a plan to execute the necessary changes. Hire, replace, retrain and realign those who need it; use the "Can & Can't, Will & Won't" matrix and develop bench strength.

While making sure that the right structure and people are in place, and that management is leading by example, implement tools and processes to monitor, measure, audit, motivate and develop the people to drive outcomes. As a leader be diligent in working to ensure people are using effective communication in all they do.

In this book, I have discussed a number of concepts, tools and processes to drive operations toward excellence, and I especially hope the reader has an increased appreciation for the critical role company culture plays in driving excellence. Without an underpinning culture that sets the stage for the organization, and a leadership that embodies that culture, the various tools and processes will be empty and ineffective.

Driving operational excellence is very much about having the intent to strive for it, sustaining the willpower to persevere and maintaining the awareness to observe, measure and adjust. Critically, it's not about just one thing, but rather about doing many of the right things, such as executing the right processes and tools the right way, and by taking an integrated approach that collectively builds positive pressure over time, which culminates in excellence and breakthrough results.

About the Author

Dominick Morizio, Jr. has over twenty-five years of international operations experience with leading companies and brands such as Yum! China, Subway, Domino's, Gloria Jean's Coffees, Boost Juice, and Blockbuster. He is fluent in Mandarin Chinese and thrives in multicultural operating environments.

The author can be reached at blazzing4@gmail.com

Printed in Great Britain
by Amazon